WB:
To Katie, Martha, and Marian, as always

JD:
To Sharon and Kristan

ISBN-13: 978-1-933212-36-4
ISBN-10: 1-933212-36-5

Library of Congress Cataloging-in-Publication Data

Bull, Webster, 1951-
A Kittery kayaker / limericks by Webster Bull ; illustrations by Jacqueline Decker.
p. cm.
ISBN-13: 978-1-933212-36-4 (alk. paper)
ISBN-10: 1-933212-36-5 (alk. paper)
1. Limericks. 2. Maine—Poetry. I. Title.

PN6231.L5B85 2007
811'.6—dc22

2007001807

Printed in Korea

Visit Jacqueline Decker on the Web at www.jdecker.com

Commonwealth Editions is an imprint of Memoirs Unlimited, Inc.,
266 Cabot Street, Beverly, Massachusetts 01915.
Visit us on the Web at www.commonwealtheditions.com

# A Kittery Kayaker

Limericks by Webster Bull

Illustrations by Jacqueline Decker

**COMMONWEALTH EDITIONS**
**Beverly, Massachusetts**

A young city slicker named Gene

Thinks to camp in The County sounds keen,

But just let him splash

In the cold Allagash

And he'll do all his camping at Bean!

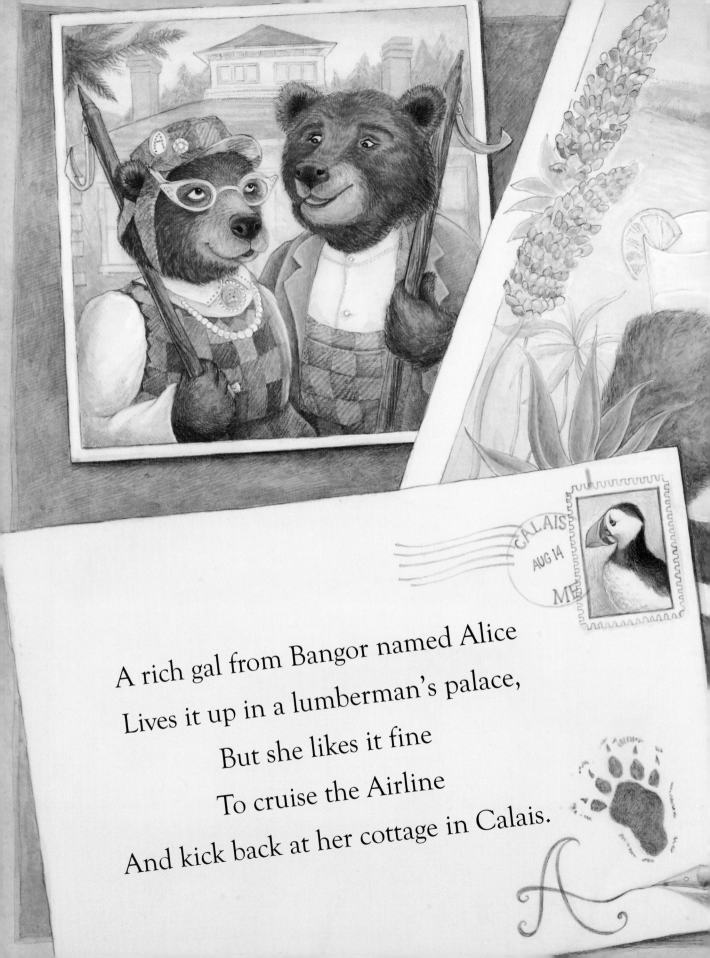

A rich gal from Bangor named Alice
Lives it up in a lumberman's palace,
But she likes it fine
To cruise the Airline
And kick back at her cottage in Calais.

René liked the mountains to ski.

Sugarloaf? Saddleback? "Ah, oui, oui!"

But a steep slope, mon Dieu,

Made him say, "Sacre bleu!

From now on ze cross-country's for me!"

A Kittery kayaker, Roddie,

Had a fit and formidable body.

He would paddle all day

From the Nubble, they say,

To the light way Down East at West Quoddy.

A man from away, name of Jud,

Thought spring starts when the daffodils bud.

"Aw, go on!" Tom cried out.

"Spring begins at ice out,

When the snow in my yard

turns to mud."

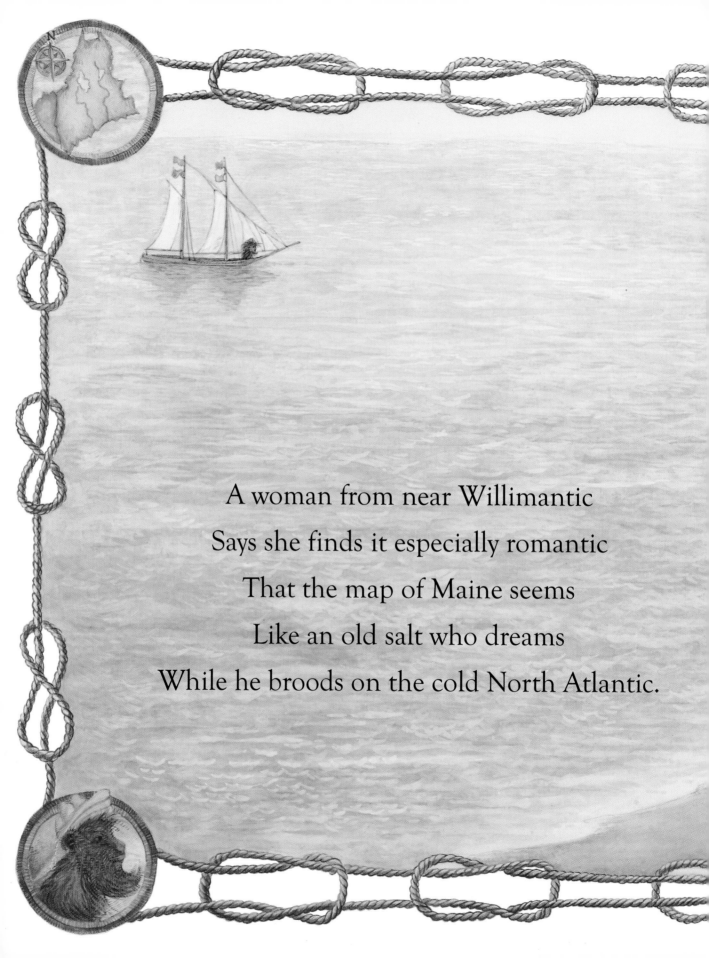

A woman from near Willimantic
Says she finds it especially romantic
That the map of Maine seems
Like an old salt who dreams
While he broods on the cold North Atlantic.

There once was a fisherman, Nate,
Who liked to use candy for bait.
On Moosehead he dropped
In a chocolate kiss—plop!
And caught a sweet mate, Mary Kate.

Penobscot

SACO
SEPT 2
ME

The rivers of Maine are a joy.
You'll love Kennebec, Saco, Seboeis,
Pisquataquis, Sheepscot,
Machias, Penobscot,
Aroostook, St. John, and St. Croix.

A yachtsman got into a stew

With a lobsterman, Freddie McGrew.

Said the rich man, "You smell!"

Said the Mainer, "Yeah, well,

'Least your nose works. I doubt that you do!"

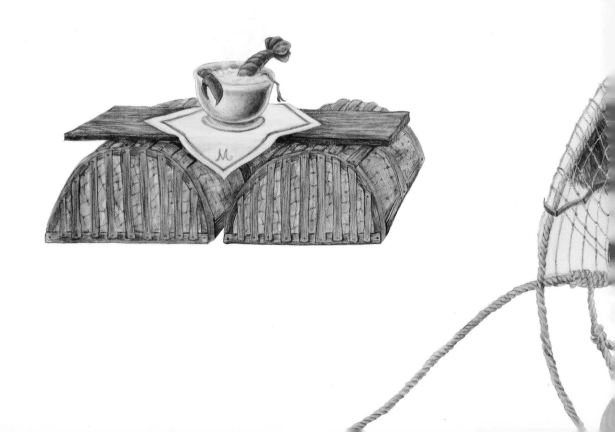

Two Portland boys, Michael and Jock,
Had grown bored sitting 'round on the dock,
So they swam to Chebeaugue, 'n
They rowed to Monhegan
Then sailed to Matinicus Rock.

A kid at Acadia Park

Read a Stephen King book in the dark.

It made him dream that

His dad was a bat

And his mom was a man-eating shark.

A girl from Township 7, Range 11,

Climbed Mt. Katahdin with her good friend Kevin.

"I can see the world!" she sighed.

"The sky is blue, and oh so wide!

This is the closest place on earth to heaven!"